A getting more customers with social media business

Growing your customer base using social media is a powerful strategy for businesses of all sizes. Here's a step-by-step guide tailored for success:

1. Define Your Target Audience

- Identify the demographics, interests, and pain points of your ideal customers.
- Understand where your audience spends their time online (e.g., Instagram, LinkedIn, TikTok).

2. Optimize Your Profiles

- Use professional profile pictures or logos.
- Write clear and engaging bios that explain who you are and what you offer.
- Include a link to your website or landing page in your bio.

3. Develop a Content Strategy

- Share content that educates, entertains, or inspires your audience.
- Use a mix of formats like videos, images, stories, and live streams.
- Incorporate user-generated content and testimonials.

4. Engage Consistently

- Respond to comments, messages, and mentions promptly.
- Join conversations in your industry or niche.
- Create polls, ask questions, and encourage audience participation.

5. Leverage Paid Ads

- Use platforms like Facebook Ads or Instagram Ads to target specific audiences.
- Run campaigns with clear goals (e.g., website visits, lead generation, sales).

6. Collaborate and Network

- Partner with influencers or other brands in your niche.
- Participate in social media challenges and trending topics.

7. Run Promotions and Contests

- Offer discounts, giveaways, or exclusive deals to attract followers and conversions.
- Use calls-to-action like "Tag a friend to win!" or "Share to enter."

8. Utilize Analytics

- Track performance metrics such as engagement, reach, and conversions.
- Use tools like Meta Insights, Google Analytics, or third-party apps to analyze data and refine your strategy.

9. Focus on Visual Appeal

- Use high-quality images and on-brand aesthetics.
- Experiment with trending formats like short-form videos (e.g., Reels, TikToks).

10. Educate and Build Trust

- Post tutorials, behind-the-scenes content, or case studies.
- Share success stories or customer reviews to establish credibility.

Example Tactics for Key Platforms:

- **Instagram**: Focus on Reels, stories, and shoppable posts.
- **Facebook**: Use groups, events, and ads to connect with local audiences.
- **TikTok**: Post creative, authentic, and trend-driven videos.
- **LinkedIn**: Share professional insights, network, and target B2B clients.

Would you like me to elaborate on any specific platform or strategic.

Defining your target audience is a critical step in creating effective social media marketing strategies. Here's how to do it:

1. Understand Your Product or Service

- What problem does it solve?
- What benefits does it offer?
- Who is most likely to need or want it?

2. Identify Demographics

- **Age**: Are they teens, young adults, middle-aged, or seniors?
- **Gender**: Is your product or service gender-specific?
- **Location**: Are they local, national, or international customers?
- **Income**: Does your product cater to specific income levels?
- **Occupation**: Are they students, professionals, entrepreneurs, etc.?

3. Analyze Psychographics

- **Interests**: What are their hobbies or passions?

- **Values**: What motivates them (e.g., sustainability, luxury, innovation)?
- **Lifestyle**: Are they fitness enthusiasts, tech-savvy, or family-focused?
- **Pain Points**: What challenges or problems do they face that your product can solve?

4. Look at Behaviors

- What social media platforms do they use?
- How do they consume content (videos, articles, images)?
- What time of day are they most active online?
- Do they prefer online shopping or in-store experiences?

5. Leverage Data

- Use tools like Google Analytics, Facebook Audience Insights, and Instagram Insights to analyze your current audience.
- Check competitors' audiences to see who they target.

6. Create Customer Personas

Develop profiles of your ideal customers, including details like:

- **Name**: "Tech-Savvy Tina" or "Budget-Conscious Bob."
- **Age and Gender**: 25–35, female.
- **Goals**: Looking for eco-friendly products.
- **Challenges**: Limited time for shopping, prefers quick and easy solutions.

7. Test and Refine

- Run small ad campaigns targeting different audience segments to see what works.
- Use feedback from your audience to better understand their needs.

Tools to Help:

- **Google Analytics** for website traffic demographics.
- **Social Media Insights** for follower data and engagement trends.
- **Surveys and Polls** to directly ask your audience about their preferences.

Defining your target audience ensures your social media efforts resonate with the right people, increasing engagement and driving results. Would you like assistance with creating a customer persona or analyzing an audience for your businesses.

Optimizing your social media profiles ensures they are professional, engaging, and aligned with your brand. Here's a detailed guide:

1. Use a Professional Profile Picture

- Choose a clear and recognizable logo or headshot.
- Ensure the image is high-quality and consistent across platforms.
- Example: If you're a business, use your logo; if you're a personal brand, use a professional photo.

---

2. Write an Engaging Bio

- **Be Concise**: Clearly explain who you are and what you offer.
- **Include Keywords**: Use words that reflect your business or industry for search optimization.
- **Show Personality**: Make it relatable and engaging.
- **Add a Call-to-Action (CTA)**: Encourage visitors to click a link or contact you.

Example Bio for a Fitness Trainer:
Helping busy professionals get fit with personalized plans. DM for free tips! 💪

---

3. Include a Link

- Use a link to direct visitors to your website, product page, or a "link-in-bio" tool like Linktree.
- Update links regularly for promotions, events, or seasonal campaigns.

---

4. Choose a Memorable Username

- Keep it consistent across platforms.
- Make it easy to spell and recognize.
- Example: Use a name like @GreenEarthCandleCo rather than @GECandles123.

---

5. Use Branded Visuals

- Create a cohesive look with consistent colors, fonts, and themes in profile pictures, cover images, and highlights.
- Example: A beauty brand might use pastel tones and minimalistic fonts.

---

6. Fill Out All Profile Sections

- **Business Information**: Add your contact info, location, and business category.
- **Services or Offers**: Highlight what you sell or provide.
- **Hours of Operation**: Especially important for local businesses.

---

7. Highlight Key Content

- Use features like Instagram Story Highlights, LinkedIn Featured Posts, or Facebook Page Tabs to showcase:
  - Top products or services.
  - Tutorials or FAQs.
  - Customer testimonials or case studies.

---

8. Optimize for SEO

- Use relevant keywords in your bio, description, and posts to make your profile discoverable.
- Example: A bakery could use terms like *"Custom Cakes | Fresh Bread | Local Ingredients"*.

---

9. Add a Pinned Post

- Pin an important post that showcases your top product, service, or announcement.
- Examples: A welcome message, new product launch, or a seasonal discount.

---

10. Stay Active and Updated

- Regularly update your profile with the latest offers, events, or achievements.
- Keep your profile photo and cover image fresh to reflect current campaigns or seasons.

Would you like help optimizing a specific social media platform like Instagram, LinkedIn, or Facebook's.

Developing a content strategy ensures your social media efforts are focused, engaging, and aligned with your business goals. Here's a step-by-step guide to crafting an effective content strategy:

---

1. Define Your Goals

- Identify what you want to achieve with your content:
  - Increase brand awareness.
  - Drive website traffic or sales.
  - Build a loyal community.
  - Educate or entertain your audience.

Example Goal: Increase website traffic by 20% in 3 months through educational content.

---

2. Know Your Audience

- Understand their interests, challenges, and preferences.
- Identify what type of content resonates with them (e.g., videos, images, blog posts).
- Use tools like audience insights from Instagram, Facebook, or Google Analytics.

---

3. Choose Your Content Types

- **Educational Content**: Tutorials, how-tos, FAQs.
- **Entertaining Content**: Memes, trending challenges, behind-the-scenes.
- **Inspirational Content**: Success stories, testimonials, quotes.
- **Promotional Content**: Discounts, product launches, giveaways.
- **User-Generated Content**: Reposting customer photos, reviews.

Tip: Maintain a balance (e.g., 70% value-driven content, 20% engagement, 10% promotional).

---

4. Select Platforms

- Focus on platforms where your target audience spends most of their time:
  - **Instagram/TikTok**: Visual and trend-focused audiences.
  - **LinkedIn**: Professional and B2B content.
  - **Facebook**: Broader demographic and community building.

---

5. Create a Content Calendar

- Plan posts in advance to ensure consistency.
- Use tools like **Trello**, **Google Sheets**, or scheduling platforms like **Buffer**, **Hootsuite**, or **Later**.
- Include dates, platforms, post captions, visuals, and CTAs.

Example Posting Schedule:

- Monday: Educational post (e.g., "5 Tips for Healthy Skin").
- Wednesday: Behind-the-scenes story.
- Friday: Promotion (e.g., "20% Off This Weekend!").

---

6. Optimize for Each Platform

- Use appropriate formats and sizes (e.g., Reels for Instagram, 16:9 for YouTube).
- Include hashtags and keywords for discoverability.
- Tailor captions to the tone of the platform (e.g., casual for TikTok, professional for LinkedIn).

---

7. Use Visuals and Branding

- Incorporate high-quality visuals and videos.
- Maintain consistent brand elements (colors, fonts, logo).
- Add captions to videos to increase accessibility.

---

8. Encourage Engagement

- Ask questions, create polls, and run contests to spark interaction.
- Respond promptly to comments and messages.
- Use call-to-actions (CTAs) like "Tag a friend," "Click the link," or "Share your thoughts!"

---

9. Measure Performance

- Track metrics like engagement rate, click-through rate, follower growth, and conversions.
- Use platform analytics or tools like Google Analytics and Sprout Social.
- Adjust your strategy based on what works best.

10. Experiment and Adapt

- Test different content types, posting times, and tones.
- Stay updated with trends and incorporate them into your strategy.
- Regularly review and refine your approach.

Would you like help creating a specific content calendar or brainstorming ideas for your business?

Consistent engagement on social media helps build trust, grow your audience, and foster a loyal community. Here's how to engage effectively and consistently:

---

1. Respond Promptly

- **Reply to Comments and Messages**: Acknowledge every comment, question, or direct message. Quick responses show your audience that you value them.
- Use a friendly and approachable tone while maintaining professionalism.

Tip: Set aside time daily for social media engagement.

---

2. Post Regularly

- Stick to a posting schedule to keep your audience engaged and your brand top of mind.
- Ideal frequency varies by platform:
    - **Instagram/TikTok**: 4–5 times a week.
    - **LinkedIn**: 2–3 times a week.
    - **Twitter/X**: 1–3 times daily.
    - **Facebook**: 3–4 times a week.

Tip: Use scheduling tools like Buffer, Hootsuite, or Later to stay consistent.

---

3. Interact with Your Audience

- **Ask Questions**: Encourage participation with open-ended questions.

- **React to User Content**: Like, share, or comment on posts where your brand is tagged.
- **Create Polls or Quizzes**: Use features like Instagram Stories or LinkedIn polls to engage directly.

---

4. Use Platform Features

- **Stories and Reels**: Share quick updates, behind-the-scenes content, or daily highlights.
- **Live Videos**: Host live Q&A sessions, product launches, or webinars.
- **Pinned Comments/Posts**: Highlight valuable conversations or announcements.

---

5. Be Authentic and Relatable

- Share personal stories or behind-the-scenes content to humanize your brand.
- Show your team, processes, or real-life uses of your products.

---

6. Engage Beyond Your Profile

- Follow relevant hashtags and join conversations.
- Comment on and share posts from industry leaders, customers, or collaborators.
- Join or create groups related to your niche (e.g., Facebook groups or LinkedIn communities).

---

7. Acknowledge User-Generated Content

- Share content your audience creates featuring your product or service.
- Thank them publicly to encourage more contributions.

Example: "We love how @UserName styled our product! ● Keep sharing your looks with #MyBrandStyle."

---

8. Run Contests and Giveaways

- Encourage likes, comments, and shares by offering prizes.
- Example: "Tag a friend and comment your favorite product for a chance to win!"

---

9. Stay Consistent with Your Brand Voice

- Use a tone that aligns with your brand's personality (e.g., friendly, humorous, professional).
- Be consistent across all interactions to reinforce brand identity.

---

10. Monitor and Adapt

- Track engagement metrics like likes, comments, and shares.
- Analyze which posts drive the most interactions and adjust your strategy accordingly.

Would you like suggestions for engagement activities specific to your industry or branch.

Leveraging paid ads on social media is a powerful way to reach a targeted audience, boost brand awareness, and drive conversions. Here's a step-by-step guide to using paid ads effectively:

---

1. Define Your Objectives

- **Set Clear Goals**:
  - Increase website traffic.
  - Generate leads or sales.
  - Boost engagement (likes, shares, comments).
  - Grow your follower base.
- Choose a specific, measurable goal for each campaign.

Example Goal: Drive 500 website visits in 2 weeks.

---

2. Choose the Right Platform

- Select platforms where your audience is most active:
  - **Facebook/Instagram Ads**: For detailed targeting and a wide range of formats.
  - **LinkedIn Ads**: Ideal for B2B marketing and professional audiences.
  - **TikTok Ads**: Best for creative, trend-driven campaigns targeting younger demographics.
  - **Google Ads**: Great for intent-driven search campaigns.

---

3. Understand Your Audience

- Use audience insights to refine targeting:
  - Demographics (age, gender, location).
  - Interests and behaviors.
  - Online habits (platform usage, activity times).
- Use tools like Meta Audience Insights or LinkedIn Analytics to gather data.

---

4. Select the Right Ad Format

- **Facebook/Instagram**:
  - Carousel Ads: Showcase multiple products.
  - Stories/Reels Ads: Short, vertical videos with high engagement.
  - Lead Ads: Collect emails directly within the platform.
- **LinkedIn**:
  - Sponsored Content: Promote posts in user feeds.
  - InMail: Send personalized messages to targeted users.
- **TikTok**:
  - In-Feed Ads: Appear within users' For You page.
  - Branded Hashtag Challenges: Encourage user-generated content.

---

5. Create Compelling Content

- Use eye-catching visuals and concise, persuasive copy.
- Include a strong **Call-to-Action (CTA)**:
  - "Shop Now," "Sign Up Today," "Learn More."
- Highlight unique selling points (USPs) of your product/service.

Example Ad Copy:
"Transform your space with our eco-friendly candles! 🌿 Shop now and get 20% off your first order."

---

6. Set Your Budget

- Choose between:
  - **Daily Budget**: Spend a set amount each day.
  - **Lifetime Budget**: Allocate a total amount for the campaign duration.
- Start small (e.g., $5–$20/day) to test performance, then scale up.

7. Use Precise Targeting

- Refine your audience based on:
  - Interests, behaviors, and purchase intent.
  - Custom audiences (e.g., retarget website visitors or email subscribers).
  - Lookalike audiences (similar to your existing customers).

8. Test and Optimize

- **A/B Testing**: Test different ad creatives, headlines, or CTAs to see what performs best.
- Analyze metrics like click-through rate (CTR), cost-per-click (CPC), and conversion rate.
- Pause underperforming ads and reallocate the budget to successful ones.

9. Retarget Your Audience

- Use retargeting ads to reconnect with users who have interacted with your brand but didn't convert.
- Examples:
  - Showcase the products they browsed.
  - Offer a discount or reminder for abandoned carts.

10. Monitor and Measure Results

- Use built-in analytics tools like:
  - **Facebook Ads Manager** or **Google Analytics** to track performance.
- Key Metrics to Monitor:
  - Impressions: How many people saw your ad.
  - Engagement: Likes, shares, clicks.
  - ROI: Revenue generated vs. ad spend.

Would you like help designing an ad campaign, crafting ad copy, or selecting a platform?

Collaborating and networking through social media can help your business expand its reach, build credibility, and attract new customers. Here's a guide to effectively collaborate and network:

---

1. Identify Potential Partners

- Look for influencers, brands, or professionals who:
  - Share your target audience.
  - Align with your brand values and goals.
  - Operate in complementary niches (not direct competitors).
- Example: A fitness trainer partnering with a nutritionist.

---

2. Build Authentic Relationships

- Engage with their content by liking, commenting, and sharing.
- DM them with personalized messages to introduce yourself and express interest in collaboration.
- Focus on creating value for both parties.

---

3. Types of Collaborations

- **Influencer Partnerships**: Work with influencers to promote your products or services through reviews, tutorials, or unboxings.
- **Brand Collaborations**: Partner with businesses to co-create content, host events, or bundle products.
- **Guest Posts or Takeovers**: Contribute content to each other's platforms (e.g., blog posts, Instagram Stories).
- **Affiliate Marketing**: Offer commission-based incentives for partners to promote your offerings.

---

4. Host Joint Events or Campaigns

- **Webinars or Live Streams**: Partner with an expert to host an informative session.
- **Giveaways**: Co-host contests with other brands or influencers.
  - Example: *"Follow both accounts, like this post, and tag 3 friends to win a prize!"*
- **Social Media Challenges**: Launch a branded challenge and invite partners to participate.

5. Utilize Local and Online Communities

- Join Facebook Groups, LinkedIn Groups, or Reddit communities related to your niche.
- Share your expertise and build connections through meaningful contributions.
- Network at virtual or in-person industry events and tag collaborators in related posts.

6. Leverage User-Generated Content

- Encourage customers and followers to create content featuring your products or services.
- Repost their content and credit them, showing appreciation and building trust.
- Example: A skincare brand sharing a customer's review video.

7. Use Hashtags and Mentions

- Tag collaborators in your posts and stories to boost visibility.
- Use niche-specific and trending hashtags to join broader conversations.

8. Share Success Stories

- Highlight past successful collaborations to attract more partners.
- Example: *"We loved working with [Influencer Name] to showcase our new product line!"*

9. Be Consistent and Genuine

- Focus on building long-term partnerships rather than one-off promotions.
- Collaborate with partners who truly believe in your product or service to maintain authenticity.

10. Track and Evaluate Success

- Use analytics tools to measure the impact of collaborations:
  - Engagement rates (likes, comments, shares).

- - Follower growth.
    - Website traffic and sales.
  - Share performance insights with your partners to strengthen the relationship and plan future projects.

Would you like help identifying potential collaborators, crafting outreach messages, or planning a specific collaboration?

Running promotions and contests on social media is an excellent way to increase engagement, grow your audience, and boost sales. Here's a guide to doing it effectively:

---

1. Set Clear Goals

- Define what you want to achieve:
  - Increase followers.
  - Drive traffic to your website.
  - Promote a new product or service.
  - Build brand awareness.

Example Goal: Gain 500 new followers and 50 new leads in one week.

---

2. Choose a Promotion or Contest Type

- **Discounts or Sales**: Offer a percentage off, "Buy One Get One Free," or flash sales.
- **Giveaways**: Reward participants with free products or services.
- **Challenges**: Encourage user participation with branded challenges (e.g., photo or video submissions).
- **Referral Campaigns**: Reward users for referring friends.

Example Contest: "Tag a friend and comment your favorite product for a chance to win!"

---

3. Define the Rules

- Keep it simple and easy to follow:
  - How to enter (e.g., like, comment, tag, or share).
  - Start and end dates.
  - Eligibility (e.g., age, location).

- Example: *"Follow us, tag 3 friends, and use #MyBrandContest to enter! Contest ends Dec. 31."*

---

4. Create an Eye-Catching Post

- Use high-quality visuals and bold text to grab attention.
- Include all essential details, like the prize, rules, and deadline.
- Add a strong **Call-to-Action (CTA)**: *"Enter now for your chance to win!"*

---

5. Offer Irresistible Prizes

- Choose a prize that excites your target audience and aligns with your brand:
  - Product bundles.
  - Gift cards.
  - Exclusive experiences (e.g., free consultations, VIP access).

Tip: Make the prize valuable enough to motivate participation.

---

6. Promote Your Contest or Sale

- Announce it across all platforms:
  - Create posts, stories, and reels.
  - Use email newsletters to inform subscribers.
- Collaborate with influencers or partners to amplify reach.
- Use paid ads to target specific audiences for better visibility.

---

7. Encourage Sharing

- Include a sharing requirement in the contest rules:
  - Example: "Share this post to your story for an extra entry!"
- Create a branded hashtag for participants to use.

---

8. Follow Up After the Promotion

- Announce the winner publicly and tag them (with permission).

- Thank all participants and encourage them to stay engaged.
- Example: *"Congrats to @Winner! And thanks to everyone who entered—stay tuned for more giveaways!"*

---

9. Measure Your Results

- Track the success of your promotion or contest:
  - Engagement: Likes, shares, and comments.
  - Follower Growth: Increase in followers during the campaign.
  - Conversions: Website visits, leads, or sales generated.

Tip: Use tools like Instagram Insights, Facebook Analytics, or Google Analytics to monitor performance.

---

10. Stay Compliant

- Follow platform-specific rules for promotions and contests:
  - Instagram: State that your contest isn't sponsored by Instagram.
  - Include disclaimers about eligibility and how winners are selected.

Would you like help creating contest ideas, crafting promotional copy, or planning a giveaways

Utilizing analytics is crucial for understanding the performance of your social media efforts, identifying what works, and refining your strategy to achieve better results. Here's a step-by-step guide to making the most of social media analytics:

---

1. Define Key Performance Indicators (KPIs)

- Determine what metrics align with your goals:
  - **Brand Awareness**: Impressions, reach, and follower growth.
  - **Engagement**: Likes, comments, shares, and saves.
  - **Website Traffic**: Click-through rate (CTR) and referral traffic.
  - **Conversions**: Leads, sales, or sign-ups.

Example Goal: Increase website traffic by 25% in 3 months through Instagram ads.

---

2. Use Built-in Analytics Tools

- Most platforms offer analytics tools:
    - **Instagram and Facebook**: Insights through Meta Business Suite.
    - **Twitter (X)**: Twitter Analytics for tweet performance.
    - **LinkedIn**: Analytics for post engagement and profile views.
    - **TikTok**: Analytics for video views and follower growth.
- Check metrics regularly to track performance trends.

---

3. Analyze Your Audience

- Understand your followers' demographics, interests, and activity:
    - Age, gender, and location.
    - Active times (best posting times).
    - Interests or behaviors.
- Use this data to refine content and targeting strategies.

---

4. Monitor Content Performance

- Identify your top-performing posts based on:
    - Engagement (likes, comments, shares).
    - Reach and impressions.
    - Saves and click-throughs.
- Assess patterns (e.g., content type, posting time) to replicate success.

---

5. Evaluate Campaign Success

- For paid ads or promotions, track:
    - Cost-per-click (CPC).
    - Return on ad spend (ROAS).
    - Conversion rate (how many users took action).
- Example: Measure whether an ad campaign drove sales or website visits.

---

6. Compare Organic vs. Paid Performance

- Assess the effectiveness of organic posts versus paid ads:
    - Which generates more engagement or conversions?

- Allocate resources to maximize ROI.

---

7. Track Trends Over Time

- Use analytics to identify long-term patterns:
    - Are engagement rates improving?
    - Is your audience growing consistently?
- Example: Monthly reports can highlight if certain months or campaigns perform better.

---

8. Experiment and Test

- Conduct A/B tests to find what works best:
    - Test different content formats (videos, carousels, static posts).
    - Experiment with captions, hashtags, or posting times.
- Analyze results and adapt your strategy.

---

9. Leverage Third-Party Tools

- Use tools for deeper insights and cross-platform analysis:
    - **Google Analytics**: Track website traffic from social media.
    - **Hootsuite**: Monitor multiple platforms in one place.
    - **Sprout Social**: Advanced reporting and analytics.
    - **HubSpot**: For lead generation and CRM integration.

---

10. Refine Your Strategy

- Use insights to:
    - Focus on high-performing platforms.
    - Create more content that resonates with your audience.
    - Adjust your posting schedule for maximum reach.
- Example: If Reels drive higher engagement, allocate more effort to video content.

Would you like help interpreting analytics from a specific platform or creating a reporting templates

Focusing on visual appeal is essential for standing out on social media, attracting attention, and reinforcing your brand identity. Here's how to create visually stunning and cohesive content:

---

1. Establish a Consistent Brand Style

- **Define Your Visual Identity**:
    - Choose brand colors, fonts, and design elements that reflect your brand personality.
    - Use the same logo or watermark across all visuals.
- **Create a Style Guide**: Document your visual guidelines to ensure consistency.

Example: A skincare brand using pastel tones, clean fonts, and soft lighting.

---

2. Invest in High-Quality Visuals

- Use sharp, professional-quality images and videos.
- For product-based businesses, showcase items with good lighting and clean backgrounds.
- Consider hiring a photographer or using editing tools to enhance quality.

---

3. Use Tools to Create Professional Designs

- Design eye-catching content with tools like:
    - **Canva**: Easy-to-use templates for social media graphics.
    - **Adobe Express** or **Photoshop**: Advanced customization.
    - **CapCut** or **InShot**: For editing engaging videos.
- Utilize templates to save time while maintaining a polished look.

---

4. Incorporate Engaging Formats

- Experiment with visually dynamic content types:
    - **Reels or TikToks**: Short, entertaining videos with transitions or trends.
    - **Carousels**: Swipeable posts for storytelling or tutorials.
    - **Infographics**: Simplify data into shareable visuals.
- Use motion graphics or animations to grab attention.

---

5. Prioritize Storytelling

- Combine visuals with captions to create a narrative:
  - Show before-and-after photos.
  - Use videos to demonstrate how your product solves a problem.
  - Share behind-the-scenes content to humanize your brand.

---

6. Keep Layouts Clean and Balanced

- Avoid cluttered designs—focus on minimalism.
- Use white space to draw attention to key elements.
- Highlight important text or CTAs with bold fonts or contrasting colors.

---

7. Adapt Content for Each Platform

- Optimize visuals to fit the dimensions and format of each platform:
  - Instagram posts: Square (1080x1080px).
  - Instagram Stories/Reels: Vertical (1080x1920px).
  - LinkedIn or Twitter: Horizontal (1200x628px).
- Use platform-specific features like stickers or filters to enhance appeal.

---

8. Use Consistent Filters and Effects

- Apply the same filter or editing style to your photos and videos to maintain brand cohesion.
- Example: A travel brand might use warm tones to evoke adventure.

---

9. Include User-Generated Content (UGC)

- Showcase authentic photos or videos from your customers.
- Encourage followers to share content featuring your brand with a unique hashtag.
- Example: Reposting customers using your product in their daily lives.

---

10. Test and Iterate

- Experiment with different styles and formats to see what resonates with your audience.
- Use analytics to identify top-performing visual content and refine your approach.

Would you like assistance designing a specific visual, planning a cohesive feed, or brainstorming creative ideas for your brand?

Educating your audience and building trust is key to forming strong, lasting relationships with your customers. By offering value, sharing knowledge, and maintaining authenticity, you can establish yourself as a credible resource. Here's how to effectively educate and build trust on social media:

---

1. Share Valuable Content

- **Provide Useful Information**: Share tips, tutorials, and how-to guides related to your industry.
  - Example: A fitness brand could post workout routines or nutrition tips.
- **Solve Problems**: Address common challenges your audience faces and show how your product or service can help.
  - Example: A skincare brand explaining how to deal with acne or dry skin.

---

2. Be Transparent

- **Show Behind-the-Scenes**: Give your audience a glimpse into your processes, whether it's how products are made or how you run your business.
- **Be Honest About Your Products**: Highlight both the benefits and limitations of your offerings to avoid over-promising.
  - Example: If you're selling a service, outline potential results while setting realistic expectations.

---

3. Share Customer Testimonials and Case Studies

- **Highlight Reviews**: Share real testimonials from customers to demonstrate the value your product or service provides.
  - Example: A software company sharing user success stories of how their tool helped improve efficiency.

- **Case Studies**: Show real-world examples of how your product has made a difference. Break down the problem, solution, and outcome.

---

4. Offer Free Resources

- **Educational Content**: Share free guides, webinars, eBooks, or workshops that provide in-depth knowledge in your field.
    - Example: A marketing agency offering a free guide on how to create effective social media ads.
- **Free Trials or Samples**: Let your audience try before they buy to build trust and allow them to see the value firsthand.

---

5. Consistent Messaging and Quality Content

- **Stay Consistent**: Post regularly and consistently on all channels to establish reliability.
- **Invest in Quality**: Make sure your content—whether it's written, visual, or video—is well-produced and professional.

---

6. Engage Authentically

- **Respond to Questions and Comments**: Take the time to interact with followers, answer questions, and provide thoughtful responses.
- **Personalize Communication**: Show your human side by addressing customers by name or tailoring responses to their specific concerns.
- **Address Criticism Constructively**: If a negative comment arises, address it calmly and professionally to show you're committed to improvement.

---

7. Educate Through Storytelling

- **Tell Your Brand Story**: Share how your brand was founded, your values, and the journey that led to your product's creation.
    - Example: A sustainable fashion brand telling the story of how they started with a vision to reduce waste.
- **Use Customer Stories**: Feature customer stories on how your product or service made a difference in their lives.

---

8. Showcase Your Expertise

- **Host Webinars or Live Sessions**: Conduct educational webinars or live Q&A sessions where you share your expertise and interact with your audience.
  - Example: A financial planner hosting a live session on budgeting tips for young professionals.
- **Guest Appearances**: Partner with industry experts for interviews or collaborative content that highlights your authority in the field.

---

9. Be Consistent with Your Brand Values

- **Stand by Your Mission**: Stick to the values that matter most to your brand and audience. If you claim to be sustainable, show it through your actions (e.g., packaging, sourcing).
- **Show Social Responsibility**: Engage in causes your audience cares about, whether it's sustainability, charity work, or community involvement.

---

10. Provide Ongoing Support

- **Create a Knowledge Base**: Share FAQs, guides, and tutorials that customers can easily access to learn more about your products or services.
- **Offer Customer Support**: Be responsive to inquiries, and provide excellent customer service to show you genuinely care about your customers' experience.

By focusing on education, transparency, and engagement, you can build a strong foundation of trust and become a go-to resource in your industry. Would you like suggestions for specific types of educational content or how to structure your customer support?